I0478701

Listening Skills

Master The Art Of Listening And Communication Skills For A More Confident Life

By

Michele Gilbert

Visit My Amazon Author Page

Dedicated to those who choose to stretch beyond their own limits to seek a more abundant and fulfilling life.

Your thoughts are creative.

Michele Gilbert

My Free Gift To You!

As a way of saying thank you for downloading my book, I am willing to give you access to a selected group of readers who (every week or so) receive inspiring, life-changing kindle books at deep discounts, and sometimes even absolutely free.

Wouldn't it be great to get amazing Kindle offers delivered directly to your inbox?

Wouldn't it be great to be the first to know when I'm releasing new fresh and above all sharply discounted content?

But why would I do something like this?

Why would I offer my books at such a low price and even give them away for free when they took me countless hours to produce?

Simple…. because I want to spread the word.!

For a few short days Amazon allows Kindle authors to promote their newly released books by offering them deeply discounted (up to 70% price discounts and even for free. This allows us to spread the word extremely quickly allowing users to download thousands and thousands of copies in a very short period of time.

Once the timeframe has passed, these books will revert back to their normal selling price. That's why you will benefit from being the first to know when they can be downloaded for free!

So are you ready to claim your weekly Kindle books?

You are just one click away! Follow the link below and sign up to start receiving awesome content

Thank you and Enjoy!

Table of contents

Introduction

I want to thank you and congratulate you for downloading the book, "Listening Skills: How To Master The Art Of Listening And Communication Skills For A More Confident Life"

This book contains proven steps and strategies on how to properly listen.

Tired of people labeling you as a forgetful person or blowing up on you for checking the score instead of listening to their story about work or a dream they had? Well, there's a reason for that. It's because you're not listening to them. Now, I know what you're thinking, listening is easy. Well, you're wrong or you wouldn't be 'that person' who everyone thinks lives in their own little world.

In fact, no matter who you are, we can all learn to listen better. Why? Because active listening is going to revolutionize your life. It's going to change the way you see others, the world around you, and how successful you are. No joke. If you want better intimacy with lovers or friends, better progress in your career, more sex, or just to be smarter and wiser; then start listening. So how exactly do you learn how to listen better? After all, you probably thought you were doing it right all along. Well you haven't been. The first step is reading this book and right now, So it looks like you've taken the first step. So keep going.

Thanks again for downloading this book, I hope you enjoy it!

CHAPTER ONE:
The Art of the Ear

Have you ever heard someone repeat the old saying that religious people have been using since someone drifted off while they were speaking? God only gave us one mouth and two ears so that we would listen twice as much. Well, I'm not an overly religious person and I'm not sure that I have the answers to the Cosmos or the greater questions in life, but I do have a response to that. It's pretty much true, in a sense.

If there is one thing that can drive a man or woman insane is the scenario that no one will listen to them. Ever want to communicate something only to have someone completely miss what you're saying? It's enough to make your hands clench into a fist and your blood boil. There's a reason for this.

There are many who believe that the greatest desire of the human being is to be understood and the key to being understood is communication. Communication brings us together, binds us, inspires us, educates us, enlightens us, and relaxes us. It's the way intimacy is build and it's the way validation is given. Without communication, we are entirely isolated in a world that we don't entirely understand and that can be stifling and terrifying to man. But the key to communication is that there are three aspects to it. Thought, vocalization, and interpretation. One is the art of the mind and how to think of things. The second is the art of the mouth and how to coin those thoughts into a medium by which we can share or test these thoughts. But for us, the focus is the art of the ear, receiving the words of others so that they might inspire our minds or that we might help them.

While we spend copious amounts of time shackled to our minds and often feel the urge to spread our ideas, thoughts, or questions; we are very diligent in neglecting the art of the ear. Our ability to truly listen and understand others is very hard, because it's something we don't always want to utilize and that becomes a problem. If you don't listen to your friends, your coworkers, or your wife; then you're destined for failure in your relationships.

That's why the art of the ear is vital for you to understand if you want to boost your relationships. So here's the rub for you. If you want to energize, invigorate your relationships, then you're going to want to take this book and study it closely because there is one thing that I can promise you. The more you utilize your ears, the more you will inspire and influence those around you to keep coming back. Those who listen more than they talk give off the aura of wisdom, intelligence, and more than that, it isn't a lie. It isn't wrong. Do you understand that? People who listen more than they talk are wise and they are intelligent. Because in the end, you'll understand that there is more to the world that you can learn by listening and the more you learn the smarter you are and the wiser you'll be come.

If you want to be a sage person and to experience life without actually having to go through the suffering and the pain of hurts and wrongs; then start listening. People will be inspired by you, they will come to you and they will invest their lives with you if they know that you're willing to truly listen to them. This is something that you're bound to find out if you just take the time to study the art of the ear.

So whether you want to inspire your coworkers, influence those around you, or find that deeper level of intimacy with your spouse, then take notes, keep an open mind, and start utilizing the things you learn here the moment you put this book down. I guarantee that you'll start seeing the differences immediately in those around you.

CHAPTER TWO:
The Ballad of the Man Who Wouldn't Listen

Now we all know someone in their life that wouldn't actually listen to them, but more importantly, we all know someone who has screwed up their life royally by not listening. Sooner or later, there's a person who gets their life completely into the dumps, sucked down in the muck until there's nothing that can really save them all because when it boils down to it, it comes down to not listening.

Seriously, that guy or that girl, they tank the perfect relationship, they lose the dream job, or they lost a friend because they were too busy not listening to actually open their ears and save themselves in time. I look at this as some of the most avoidable sufferings and sorrows in the world. There are a lot of people out there who sink their lives because they don't deal with what's going with themselves. They don't deal with the simple fact that they are the people screwing up their lives and they assume that it's some cosmic joke that they're suffering.

Do not be this man. Do not be that woman. Be the person who is present in their lives. Be the person that knows what's going on in their day to day events and avoid the suffering that's needlessly enters some peoples' lives. I want you to take a moment to see if your life for what it really is. Moments.

Life is full of moments. Moments of silence, moments of excitement, moments of stress, and moments of opportunity, and countless other moments. For each moment that you experience in your life, there are people around you or you are alone. Now take stock of those moments in your day to day experience, seeing how much time you spend alone, how much time you spend with people, and when you're with people, how much time do you spend actually listening versus waiting to talk to them.

For people who sink their lives because a lack of communication, the reality is that they're probably not actually listening to the people around them. They're not listening to their spouses, to their friends, to their coworkers, or the average people that they run into day to day. When you're with them and communication is initiated, do you simply wait as they talk, forming your next sentence, or do you take the time to digest their words, pondering them before you respond? How do you navigate conversations?

Seriously, take a moment to think it over!

Are you a person who actually listens? Do you know how to listen? Or are you one of those people who don't listen and watches time and time again as miscommunications, 'forgetful' moments, or being on the wrong page consumes your relationships and leaves you alone and misunderstanding how things got to this point? This is an honest question that you need to ask yourself. Are you a person who doesn't know how to listen? Because if you know the answer to that, then you know that you can change it.

Remember that other old saying: the first step to solving any problem is acknowledging that there is one. Remember that? Well I think that one has truth to it as well and that you can seriously take charge of your life by actually adjusting the way you listen to people and good news. The first step down having a richer, deeper communication in life is by reading this book. So you're already on the right path, so keep going.

CHAPTER THREE:
Avoiding Misunderstandings

One hundred percent of the time there's a misunderstanding is that there was not clear communication. That is a fact. There is no way that there can be a misunderstanding of both people are fully communicating, dedicating one hundred percent of their thoughts and their focus on the person they were talking to. This isn't a magical or secret in life. If you're not focusing on what someone is saying to them, you're not going to absorb what they're saying by audible osmosis. That's not a thing.

What is a thing is listening.

Feel like you're reading a book about reinventing the wheel? That listening is easy and that only a moron couldn't do this? Well an average statistic that is thrown around by psychologists is that on average, 75% of the time we're supposed to be listening, we're actually distracted or preoccupied which leads to the big lie that you 'forgot' what that person told you. Did you know that the majority of people listen in order to respond to what is being said to them, not to actually understand the information they're receiving? That's not listening. Did you know that on a list of major and prominent problems polled from husbands and wives across America, regardless of gender, sexual preference or age, that better communication is always in the top five things that people would like in their relationship? We're talking overwhelming majorities here. But wait; let's drive this home professionally as well. Did you know that during interviews, most major corporations study applicants for listening skills to determine whether they have truly developed communication skills rather than knowing how to respond to an interview or work an interview?

Let's talk about forgetting now, for a moment. And let me throw some sarcastic quotation marks around it. "Forgetting." Catch my drift? The truth is that the majority of the things you "forget" that your wife/husband told you, or that appointment to hang out that you blew off, or one of the countless things that slipped through the cracks, probably ended up there because you weren't actually listening to that person when they were talking to you. You weren't focusing on them. You didn't misunderstand them and you didn't forget them. You just didn't invest a priority in them. That might sound cold, but you gave a text, someone attractive walking by, thoughts about something else, or any numerous distractions priority over what was being communicated to you. Seriously, think about it. Sure, there are times you genuinely forget, because it gets steam rolled by other things, but most of the time it's actually you "forgot."

So reinventing the wheel might be exactly what we need right now.

The key to avoiding misunderstanding is to hack off the mis and actually understand someone. Understanding is not hearing what they're saying and processing that into how to fix it, how to respond to it, or how to multitask while in a conversation. Understanding someone is focusing on them and giving them one hundred percent of your thought and mental power. By actually focusing on them, your mind is going to be processing things like, reasons behind it, how to apply this to your life/morals/schedule/etc., their intentions, and how this is actually affecting them. By focusing on a person and truly hearing what they're telling you, you will pick up far more information than you would by simply trying to form your response and thinking of when they're talking as dead time to postulate. No, understanding requires focus and mental dedication to what is being communicated to you.

Try this on your next conversation. Actually listen to the person you're speaking to. Invest your focus on them and actually listen to what they're saying, how they're saying, discern why they're saying it, and why this is important to them. No one communicates worthless facts and statements, even when it seems random it's not. You can learn so much about people by what they say to you. So when you communicate with someone next, focus on them and understand them.

CHAPTER FOUR:
The Slave of the Machine

Welcome to the twenty first century! Welcome to the future. Here are your zillion social network accounts. Here's your home email, your shopping email, your work email, and a thousand different online accounts. Here's your cellphone and hundred contacts that are going to text you daily or annually. Here are your updates on your favorite movies, sports teams, bands, etc. Here's live streaming of television everywhere and here's a billion distractions that your grandparents' minds didn't have to combat and struggle with for attention. Welcome to the mental meat grinder.

We are slaves to technology. It's plain and simple and technology is a lovely master or mistress. No question about it. But it is murder on your physical, flesh and blood relationships. If you need proof of this and don't necessarily want to look in the mirror, then head to the nearest coffee shop or restaurant and when you've sat down and got comfortable, look around. You will notice how many people are on laptops, checking their phones, talking on their phones, or simply playing games on their phone. There's nothing about this that is healthy, especially when you're with other people. In fact, you'll even see groups of people, all of them on their phones.

Now, yes, phones are great tools and resources to make life easier, but they shouldn't govern your life. If you can't experience conversations without having your phone out or being able to be in the moment, then you have a problem. Now, don't be scared or feel like you're alone here, because there are thousands that have the same problem as you and it's the fact that so many are leashed to the virtual world. So there's definitely a problem, but what does that mean? What should you do about this to break free?

Well, with anything, it always starts with baby steps and this baby step is to acknowledge that there are vital resources that we utilize with our cellphones and then there are frivolous resources that we use. Know the difference. If someone is trying to call you from your work, then that's important. So is a phone call or text from family, loved ones, or close friends that need you in the moment. Everything else, it's excessive and it's recreational. So take a moment and see what's vital and what isn't when it comes to your cellphone.

Once you know what your priorities are, then it's easy to see where you can cut back. Know that you have dead time to look at sport scores, news stories, band updates, movie trailers, etc. Think about all the time that you have alone to go over that stuff and organize your life accordingly. That way, when you sit down with others, it's easy for you to take the next step.

And that step is to focus on the person you're with. Don't waste this time with someone because they're in that moment with you for a reason. Either they love you or they like you, or they need you, and they're there to experience something with you, not let you whittle the time away checking your Facebook. In reality, unplugging is one of the best things you can do for your life and the relationships around you.

In the last chapter, we discussed how important it is to be focused on those that you're with and how you really need to invest the mental energy in truly understanding a conversation to get the most out of it. So cut away the distractions that are poisoning your ability to truly be there with the people around you. You'll immediately notice the difference and so will others. It's just good manners and it will really start to bug you when you notice that others don't have the same level of respect.

So don't be a slave to the machines in your life. The Internet is bringing the world closer and closer with each passing day, but at the expense of those right in front of you. Show some respect and start to unplug. You'll see the difference almost immediately in the relationships around you and closest to you. People will feel more valued if you sit next to them and turn your phone off, or at least on vibrate. Baby steps remember. Baby steps.

CHAPTER FIVE:
The Accusation of Not Listening

Everyone in their lives has been accused of not listening and that's usually the beginning of a fight or a problem that could have been avoided, much like we've discussed earlier. So we've learned why listening is important in this book. How not listening can lead to unwanted and unneeded complications. How focus is vital to actually communicating clearly and fully with others. And we also discussed the importance of unplugging and truly being present in those conversations in your day to day life. Now, let's take a moment and discuss why people get angry when you're not listening.

We know that it happens. If you need proof of it, next time you're with your spouse or partner or person of interest, just sort of zone out. You will watch the wrath of that person descend upon you with unholy speed and vengeance. Of course, do this at your own peril. Actually, just take my word for it and save yourself some hurt.

But why? Why do people care so much whether you're listening or not? Especially if what's being communicated is really trivial or pointless. Let's be honest, people usually don't like hearing about dreams they weren't in or weren't very interesting. They don't like hearing about tedious work stories that really don't have a point. We don't actually care about what happened in traffic. But that's not the point.

You should. Especially if you're in a committed relationship, because that person is invested in you and has allowed you access to their life. People who talk to you have some sort of investment in your life as well and they want to share the events of their lives with you because they feel an intimacy with you that they don't find in others. This is usually an exclusive club that you're in and you should handle it with respect. They care about you and they want you to know that something happened to them.

No matter how tedious you think it is, it isn't. If you're hearing a work, traffic, or other story that you're not in, they're not telling it to you because you're their diary. They're telling it to you because they have an emotional investment in the event that unfolded in their lives. This is being told to you for a reason, so listen to them, and focus on the details of how and why they're telling you this.

Because in the end, that's what being a genuinely good person is.

Let's boil that sentence down a bit and come at it from another angle. If you're just approaching every relationship and conversation in your life with the "What am I getting out of this?" approach, then you are a selfish person and probably need to work on your basic humanistic presence. Most people will consider you a jerk because all you care about is proving a point, venting, or thinking of how to respond to someone, not actually caring in their situations and their problems. Don't be that person. Seriously, do not be that person.

The person talking to you needs your help wants you to fulfill something, have the support of a friend, or they love you and want to experience life with you. All of these reasons are perfectly valid ways to go about your life and you shouldn't forsake them lightly. In fact, you should relish the fact that you are communicating with people and act accordingly.

So why are people trying to communicate with you? Because they're investing their lives with you and that is a rare honor that shouldn't be taken lightly. So why are they mad when you're not listening or letting your mind wander from distraction to distraction? Because you are disrespecting their investment and showing them that the level of trust, interest, or love that they have placed in you is not equal and that you have more important things on your mind.

This is never true, so don't believe it, but that's what you're communicating to them. You're just being lazy and disrespectful whether you are doing so intentionally or not. So if you're still wondering why this matters, then reread this chapter before moving on and start implementing what you've learned before the next step. So start showing some respect, love, and interest in those around you.

CHAPTER SIX:
How to Inspire Interest

So now that you have some foundational steps in how to become a better listener. How do you apply this professionally? Maybe you don't have a spouse that you want to reach a deeper level of intimacy with. Maybe you're more of the career driven/oriented people of the world and you need people to stop thinking that you don't care about their ideas. Maybe you need to be seen as more of a team player. So how can listening put you on the path to having a more fruitful and successful business career?

Easily.

More than ever, listening is crucial in the world of business and that's because people are being consumed by the technology boom. With more email and texting, the art of having a successful face to face is getting eaten away by people checking their email and watching for texts. Meetings are more and more popular and that means sitting in small rooms with a bunch of men droning about things that may not concern or interest you, but paying attention gets noticed.

So here are some ways to use active listening to blow up your career into a new tier of success:

I. Active Listening:

When it comes to bosses, there's nothing they love more than knowing that the orders they're issuing and the tasks they need done are getting accomplished by people who are fully committed, fully understanding, and on their team. By standing by silently nodding, that means nothing to your boss. Engage in the discussion. Ask questions, raise your hand, and make yourself known and that you're invested in the task at hand. Your boss will notice your enthusiasm and interest. Don't ask stupid questions, however. Ask real questions that will give you a deeper understanding or will help you accomplish your task better. This is known as active listening. Show your boss that you're engaged.

II. Stop, Collaborate, and Listen:

Vanilla Ice has it right. When it comes to your coworkers, do not seek to dominate, but seek to accomplish. By listening to the ideas and interests of your coworkers on projects without the intention of converting them to your cause, they will feel closer to you. Not only will this give you the edge in understanding where your coworkers are, who is as invested as you are, or who has the truly better idea; but it will build closeness between you and those you work with. Having a network of equals is handy, especially as you all move on in your careers. So build that energy and that sense of community between you and your coworkers.

III. I'm not an employee. I'm an asset:

There's a difference between employee and asset. Do you know the difference? Employees are expendable. Employees are replaceable. Remember the art of the mind, mouth, and ear? Well the ear feed into the mind and that leads to knowledge. That leads to power. Remember that saying: Knowledge is power? Well that one is true too. If you want to learn, become more valuable, and become invaluable, then start listening and absorbing as much information as you can. This will show your boss that you know what you're doing, you're invested in your company, and that you're willing to do what is necessary to keep pushing forward. That's how you're going to distinguish yourself from your coworkers.

IV. The Power of Three:

Okay, so once you feel the strength and the foundation in all of these three, combine them and watch what happens. Not only will your boss feel like you're competent and if you do your assignments to perfection you will be; but your coworkers will be inspired by you because they feel valued by your investment in listening to their ideas, and you will be an indispensable asset to the company. All of this will come together with a powerful effect. If you perform accordingly and do a wonderful job at all of your tasks, then you will be unstoppable and you will be seen as the ultimate team player. Unleashing one of these tasks will benefit your life, but combining the three of them will make your professional life profoundly successful.

Don't expect immediate results, but do notice the changes with every conversation. As you talk with more and more people, fully communicating with them, whether your employer or your coworkers, you'll see changes in how they act around you. So start making the changes on Monday. Make your professional life something that is truly invested and beautiful and people will notice.

CHAPTER SEVEN:
The Way of Intimacy

Maybe you're not really worried about your career or you're in a place that you love, but your problem is that you're one of the people who wish that they had better communication in your romantic endeavors. If that's you and your partner or spouse is constantly furious with your forgetfulness or your drifting, then that might be one of the more stressful things happening in your life. But that's okay, because there's definitely a way to fix that. Listening can drastically transform your life and relationships and here's how.

It breeds intimacy.

That simple. A successful relationship isn't measured in years together or amount of sex or even how happy you are. A successful relationship is defined solely on the level of intimacy that has been achieved by the couple. Why intimacy? Because everything follows behind intimacy. Want more sex? Get intimate. Want to have a long marriage? Get intimate. Want to feel happier and satisfied with your relationship? Get intimate. Intimacy is the indicator that you are doing things right. We all know what intimacy is and if you don't, you'll recognize it when you feel it. It's the sense of oneness, the closeness of souls, the need to talk, even if it's about nothing, the urge to rip their clothes off, to harness tender moments, and a million other wonderful experiences. All of this passes through the gates of intimacy. So how do you inspire greater intimacy? How do you take the way of intimacy?

I. Start actively listening:

Just like the professional session, it all starts by actively listening. Understand that your spouse, partner, or boyfriend/girlfriend wants to feel like they're valued by you and in order to show that, you need to be engaged when they're talking. Ask questions, support them, and make them a priority. If you're distracted by something important, share it with them so they don't feel undervalued. Actively listening to the person you love will tell them that you're a priority to me. That's a way to draw someone closer to you and its genuine.

II. The Art of Anticipation:

By knowing what's important to the person you love doesn't just magically happen. You don't absorb their troubles, worries, likes, loves, and dreams by just standing next to them. You only learn these things by listening to them and that helps you known when something important comes up in their life or if something rough is on the horizon, you can be supportive for them. This shows them that you know what's going on, you care about their struggles, and that you're there with them in their day to day events. No one wants to be alone and they love you, so love them back.

III. Reciprocation Encourages:

By knowing that what they've told you and what they say to you is important to you, your loved ones are encouraged to draw closer to you and to continue their pursuit in investing in you. You want this, because that closeness is how intimacy is born and that shows them how much you love them. So if you want your loved one to keep sharing their life with you, listening and showing them that you're there, that you're with them, it'll only breed more intimacy. So encourage them to keep sharing and keep showing them that you love them. It'll only get better and better.

By pursuing the way of intimacy, your relationships will feel like they're only burgeoning more and more with every day. You will find new things out about your closest friend and companion. You will understand them and anticipate their needs. By building and investing in your spouse or partner, you'll be distinguished in their mind. They will tell you that you're the only person they've ever dated who truly listened to them or understood them. It's a sad truth that they might be right. So show them respect and love and show them that they're not disposable, that you truly love them and are invested in their lives. This will breed all the intimacy for a successful relationship.

CHAPTER EIGHT:
The Core of Communication

There are many who have studied language, communication, and listening to fully express the importance and the necessity of listening. The more we come to understand how humans communicate and how ideas are spread, the more important listening becomes to us. Listening is more than an action. It's a cognitive process of dissecting, digesting, comprehending, and establishing thoughts and events as valid or invalid in our lives. Only by listening can our lives open up to newer and more wonderful possibilities than we originally had. In truth, listening is the core of all communication.

So you've learned why listening in communication is important, some steps to start listening better, and how it can improve your relationships and your career, so start employing what you've learned. Hopefully you already have. You'll be able to see the changes in your relationships because people will treat you differently when you listen more than you speak. They will feel like they're in the presence of someone smart, wise, and sage. They will seek your opinions, your thoughts, your responses, and your viewpoints on matters. Listening is how you grow in wisdom and intelligence and you'll be surprised at the own effects on your life.

Now, before we part ways, here are some last tips.

First of all, take baby steps. Sure, some people are going to drone on about things that feel meaningless and in the end, it probably is. But remember that everyone shares something for a reason. By listening, you can probably discern the reason for their discontent or interest in what happened.

Secondly, be aware of how much you're speaking or where your mind is. Remember that distractions are the enemy and that sometimes we're our own worst enemies. If you feel like you're dominating the conversation, step back and listen to them. Start asking them questions to encourage them to talk more. Remember that the way to keep you from talking too much is to ask more questions. People love answering them and sharing.

Thirdly, unplug. Seriously, if you ask anyone who has done it and they'll tell you how vastly their life has increased and grown in richer quality. It's not a conspiracy. You'll feel happier, find focusing easier, and realize that you have more time to invest in others if you unplug. Take some baby steps or go full on cold turkey; whatever you need to do, but cut back in some form. It will make your conversations deeper, richer, and listening will be so much easier.

Finally, envision yourself as the person that you want to be. IF you want to be a better person through listening, then picture it and start acting like it. Sure, it might feel like you're playing pretend for a while, but that's how change starts. By taking on the personality of a person you want to be, you will inevitably become that person. So picture who you want to be: A better listener. And then start acting like it. Don't give up on it and as you watch the changes happening in your life, you'll be encouraged to continue on in this journey.

So if you're here at the end, looking for one thing to take away after skipping through the entire book, then take this away. Start listening to the people in your life, because they're investing in you and they clearly care about you.

Now please go back and read the book.

Conclusion

Thank you again for downloading this book!

I hope this book was able to help you understand the importance of listening

Now, you know some key strategies for keeping your communication with others healthy and vibrant.

.

Remember to continually invest in open and honest communication skills and really listen..

The next step is to take action …

Before you go, I'd like to say thank you for purchasing my book.

I know you could have picked many other books on listening skills.

 So A Big thanks for downloading this book and reading it all the way to completion.

Now I would like to ask a small favor.

Could you please take a minute or two to leave a review for this book on Amazon?

The feedback will help me continue to publish more kindle books that will help people to get better results in their lives.

And if you found it helpful in anyway then please let me know :-)

Thank you and good luck!

Preview of My New Book

Body Language 101

What A Person's Body Language Is Really Telling You... And How You Can Use It To Your Advantage

Talk to the Hand

I don't know about you, but when I watch shows like *Lie to Me* or *Sherlock*, so often, I really, really wish that I could be that good. Heck, after I watched *The Mentalist* for the first time, I was studying everyone. stared at footprints trying to see if I could tell whether the person walking was right handed or left handed Not only is this super impractical for me as an actual skill, but it's super addicting. The thing is, it's all about studying people and watching them, but there's a science to it. I may not be out there catching criminals red-handed for having a nervous tell, but it has helped me read situations and understand things that I previously missed.

So sure, you might not catch your arch-nemesis, but you might be able to understand things a little better with a little study of body language. And that's why I'm here. Body language is not just for detectives out there looking to catch murderers and thieves. Body language is the key to understanding the unspoken words that our body is communicating so heavily without our knowledge. Not only will this help you understand and relate to people better, but it'll make it so that you are aware of your own presence to others.

Nonverbal communication makes up the majority of our communication and most of us are clueless to the actual comprehension and understanding of it. That means that those who do not invest time in learning what to say in our nonverbal appearance are missing so much. But the truth is, we don't miss all of it. We have come to silently absorb and understand nonverbal communication, regardless of whether we know it or not It's the art of learning to understand something we already know and to heighten our understanding and acceptance of what's being communicated to us. It's tricky, I know, but it's not impossible to understand.

What I'm going to tell you in this book is going to make sense to you and a lot of it is going to feel familiar like you already knew that. Well, the reason for that is that you you've been picking up these silent transmissions for years, you just haven't acknowledged them or put a name to some of the habits you've already taught yourself.

So stick around and start to see if you can't agree or relate to some of the information you're going to receive. But more importantly, I want to address your homework before we start getting into the gritty, deep stuff. For instance, I want you to start watching people around you.

Observation is the birth of understanding and without a true sense of observance or a keen eye for noticing the little things, you're not going to pick up on some of these traits. When someone is talking to you, you're going to need to start watching them. Notice how they're standing, note the posture, have you looked at their eyes, what about the overall harmony of their face, and what are they doing with their hands? All of these things need to be running through your mind to really catch what is being conveyed to you. But not just watching their body, note the tones they're using, and the words that they're selecting. These are all going to tell you what sort of body language comes with certain attitudes and emotions. It all ties together and it is all relevant when it comes to understanding body language. So start opening your eyes and let's have a look at what they're trying to say to you.

Are you ready?

Weapons of Mass Induction

Though Sherlock Holmes often touts his use of deductive reasoning, it is actually the opposite that we're going to focus on with you, because right now, you're a student. For those of you that do not know, inductive reasoning starts with observations that slowly build a pattern that you will then form into hypothesis until it is proven right or wrong. If you're right, then you have a theory.

For example, Kayla touches her hair a lot when she talks to Hot Mike, but not when she's talking to anyone else. So, every time I see Kayla talking to Hot Mike and she's touching her hair, that might be a cue that she likes Hot Mike. So, until I'm proven wrong, I'm certain that I have a theory that when a woman likes a man she'll touch her hair unconsciously.

Viola, you have just jumped from observation to theory until proven wrong. Of course, when you're Sherlock Holmes level, you'll be using the art of deductive reasoning which starts at a theory and then tested with a hypothesis and observations until you have a conclusion. I think it's time for another example to prove this one to you.

Click Here To Read The Rest of

Body Language 101

What A Person's Body Language Is Really Telling You... And How You Can Use It To Your Advantage

P.S. You'll find many more books like this and others under my name Michele Gilbert.

Don't miss them... here is a short list.

Wicca: The Ultimate Beginners Guide For Witches and Warlocks: Learn Wicca Magic

The Introvert's Advantage: The Introverts Guide To Succeeding In An Extrovert World

Stop Playing Mind Games: How To Free Yourself Of Controlling And Manipulating Relationships

Instant Charisma: A Quick And Easy Guide To Talk, Impress, And Make Anyone Like You

Chakras: Understanding The 7 Main Chakras For Beginners: The Ultimate Guide To Chakra, Mindfulness, Balance and Healing

Practicing Mindfulness: Living in the moment through Meditation: Everyday Habits and Rituals to help you achieve inner peace

Adrenal Fatigue: What Is Adrenal Fatigue Syndrome And How To Reset Your Diet And Your Life

About Michele Gilbert

Michele Gilbert was born and raised in Brooklyn, New York. Drawn to literature and writing at a young age, she enrolled at Brooklyn College and majored in English. After graduation Michele did not begin writing immediately, instead she embarked on a career in the finance industry and spent the next thirty years on Wall Street.

Serendipity struck when she least expected it. After ending a long-term relationship, Michele found herself lost and unsure what the future held. She began to read books on grief and loss, looking for answers. Those led her to delve deeper into the Law of Attraction and its power. What resulted was remarkable. Not only had she begun to heal, she had also rekindled her former love of writing and discovered her life's purpose.

The years have taken her through many twists and turns, but she learned valuable lessons along the way. Today she publishes books-mostly self-help and metaphysical in nature-and feels compelled to share her knowledge with those facing similar experiences. Her greatest hope is to inspire others and show them ways to overcome adversity and gracefully accept life's inevitable low points.

Going forward, she plans to incorporate more teachings of self-help, finance and meditation. Regular meditation is very beneficial to her progress as she forges a new life. Morning rituals and positive incantations are other practices Michele embraces; they are very restorative in daily life.

As an avid hiker, Michele and fellow club members often hike the picturesque Jersey Pine Barrens. She is a history buff, voracious reader, baseball fanatic and a foodie. She also proudly supports Trout Unlimited-a national non-profit organization dedicated to conserving, protecting and restoring North America's Coldwater fisheries and their watersheds.

Michele currently resides forty minutes from Atlantic City and the Jersey Shore. She makes her home with a Blue Russian rescue cat named Jersey, though she isn't exactly sure who rescued who.

Michele really enjoys publishing books that can make a difference in people's lives. If you have any suggestions or would like to have a specific topic covered in a future book, please send an email to michelegilbertbooks@gmail.com and we will get back to you.

Thanks for reading!

www.ingramcontent.com/pod-product-compliance
Lightning Source LLC
Chambersburg PA
CBHW041614180526
45159CB00002BC/852